Snap
books®

Synchronized Skating

BY MARY E. SCHULTE

Consultant:
Kristin Eberth
United States Figure Skating double gold medalist
Professional figure skater with Disney On Ice

CAPSTONE PRESS
a capstone imprint

Snap Books are published by Capstone Press,
1710 Roe Crest Drive, North Mankato, Minnesota 56003
www.mycapstone.com

Library of Congress Cataloging-in-Publication Data
Cataloging-in-Publication data is available on the Library of
Congress website.
ISBN 9781515781868 (library binding)
ISBN 9781515781905 (eBook PDF)

Editorial Credits
Brenda Haugen, editor; Veronica Scott, designer; Kelli Lageson,
media researcher; Kathy McColley, production specialist

Photo Credits
Dreamstime: Anna Krivitskaia, 15 (bottom), Canonman29, 24, Nicholas
Piccillo, 12; Getty Images: Amy Sussman, 28, ISU/Daniel Kopatsch,
27, ISU/Dave Sandford, 7 (middle left), Jared Wickerham, 9, 14, The
Boston Globe/Joanne Rathe, 21; Newscom: Icon Sportswire/Fred
Kfoury III, 5; Shutterstock: Aija Lehtonen, 7 (top right, middle right,
bottom), 8, 11, anfisa focusova, 3, Bojan Milinkov, 17, Grekov's, 15,
TopJan Faukner, cover, 29, Photoman29, 6, 7 (top left), 10, 16, 18, 19, 20,
22, 23, Shooter Bob Square Lenses, cover, throughout

Design elements: Shutterstock

Printed and bound in Canada.
010395F17

Table of Contents

Introduction

In Sync

Imagine gliding forward, balanced on one foot. Your other foot is raised behind you **parallel** to the ground as you spin in a circle. Now imagine doing it wearing ice skates. To make it even harder, think about performing the move at exactly the same time and at the same speed as up to 19 other skaters. That is synchronized skating.

Synchronized skating is the newest and fastest growing type of figure skating. **Precision skating** has been around since the 1950s, but the first World Synchronized Skating Championship (WSSC) was in 2000. Now more than 600 teams are registered with the U.S. Figure Skating Association.

Each team has eight to 20 people. Most teams are made up of girls, but boys can compete too. Synchronized skating involves teamwork, speed, complicated **formations**, and challenging **step sequences**.

parallel—an equal distance apart

precision skating—the original name for synchronized skating

formation—the way in which members of a group are arranged

step sequence—a set of moves that follow one after the other

Chapter 1

The Basics

Synchronized skaters build their routines around five basic **elements**. The elements include blocks, circles, wheels, lines, and intersections. Beginning skaters perform these formations and focus on keeping straight lines and holding onto one another. Teams are required to perform step sequences with turns.

element—a required move in synchronized skating

THE 5 BASIC ELEMENTS:

blocks

circles

wheels

intersections

lines

7

But you won't see any double axels by young skaters. Only at the advanced levels can they add spins, jumps, and lifts. As their skills grow, teams' formations become more complex. They increase in difficulty and creativity and include more required elements.

Twizzles

Have you ever heard of a twizzle? A twizzle is a spin in which skaters rotate on one foot while still moving forward. Twizzles can be fast or slow, forward or backward. When you see a whole line of skaters performing a twizzle at the same time, it looks amazing!

MAKE YOUR MOVE

At the advanced competitive levels, the programs also include various required elements. These include a pairs element, group lift, combined element, synchronized spin, no-hold element, creative element, and move element. During the move element, the whole team connects in different variations to perform a "move in the field," such as a spread eagle. A spread eagle is a graceful move where a skater glides on both feet with the toes pointed out and heels facing each other.

a spread eagle

Chapter 2

Moving on Up

U.S. synchronized teams are divided into 14 levels according to the age and skill level of the team members. Two divisions are for college teams. Some of the best teams come together at college.

Among the 14 competitive levels are the juvenile, intermediate, novice, junior, senior, collegiate, adult, and masters levels. These teams compete at the regional level, then at the sectional level. If a team places in the top four at sectionals, it can compete at the national level in the U.S. Synchronized Skating Championships.

The best teams are perfectly synchronized.

A team performs lifts.

The best teams at the junior and senior levels can earn a place on the U.S. Synchronized Skating Team. The top two senior teams represent the United States at the WSSC. The team that wins is the best in the world.

Fast Fact

In the 1990s there were just four college teams in the United States. By 2016, 36 competed in the collegiate and open collegiate divisions.

TESTING

If a skater wants to compete, he or she has to pass a test. A judge watches and grades the skater. Tests are marked "passed" or "retry." Many top skaters have to take a test more than once to pass.

A student must pass a test to advance to the next level. As a skater moves up to the next level, the tests get harder. The highest achievement is passing the senior or gold test. When a skater passes a gold test, he or she earns the title "U.S. Figure Skating gold medalist."

Good synchronized skaters need to be strong in dance, free skate, and even pairs. Most senior-level synchronized team skaters have passed a gold test in at least two of five skill areas called tracks. Each skater improves at his or her own pace, but it usually takes at least 10 years of hard work and practice to reach a gold test level.

FIVE FIGURE SKATING TRACKS

Moves in the Field:

This tests skating skills. Moves in the Field has eight levels. Each level has four to six patterns the skater must perform. Each level builds on the skills learned in the previous level.

Pairs:

This test has six levels. Pairs tests are most often taken by teams that want to compete in qualifying events.

Pattern Dance and Solo Pattern Dance:

This test requires steps to music, skated in a certain tempo, or speed. There are eight levels. Each level includes three or four dances. Skaters can perform with a partner or can test in the solo track.

Free Skate:

This tests a skater's abilities in required jumps, spins, and steps. Free skate tests have the same eight levels as Moves in the Field. A skater may not attempt a free skate test until they pass the Moves in the Field test for that level. As the levels go up, the length of the program increases along with the number of required elements. Presentation is also judged.

Free Dance and Solo Free Dance:

This tests programs to music and includes lifts, spins, step sequences, and synchronized twizzles. There are five levels in this track. The solo free dance has different required elements to allow a skater without a partner to participate.

Chapter 3

Preparing to Be the Best

Why do figure skaters choose synchronized skating? Many like to work together as a team. Each skater gets to work on his or her own skills and bring those skills to the team.

Off the ice, synchronized skating teams practice **choreography** and counting their steps. Practicing hundreds of steps, wearing tennis shoes instead of skates, the teammates count the beats and mark the steps to their music. When it's time to perform, they make it look easy.

A team is only as good as its weakest link. So while the skaters may practice together on the ice twice a week, they also have to practice by themselves. Skaters take private lessons to improve their skills. That can be an added expense. But often the biggest expense for team members is high-quality skates, which can cost up to $1,000.

choreography—the arrangement of steps, movements, and required elements that make up a synchronized skating routine

Figure Skates

Some synchronized skaters use different skates than other skaters use. The blade on a figure skate has a hollow groove on the bottom. This creates two distinct edges, the inside edge and the outside edge. Skaters glide on one edge of the blade at a time. Some synchronized skaters use dance blades. Dance blades are about 1 inch (2.5 centimeters) shorter than those on singles skates. The shorter blades help make turns easier.

GETTING IN SHAPE

You might think skating is all about the legs. But in synchronized skating, **core** strength and upper-body strength help the skaters stay connected in a line. Skaters must also have good balance and **flexibility**.

Synchronized skating routines are only a few minutes long, but skaters work hard and skate fast. Their hearts need to be strong. Lifting weights helps skaters grow stronger. Running builds **endurance**. Skaters often take yoga classes for flexibility and ballet classes to learn dance moves.

The U.S. Figure Skating Association recommends a variety of exercises for skaters. It's also a good idea to have a trainer or coach guide your exercise program.

Core and upper-body strength, as well as balance and flexibility, are needed for synchronized skating.

Helpful Exercises

Various exercises help with different skills. For example, a skater needs good balance. Balance is the ability to keep your **center of gravity** over your base of support. The wider your base, the easier it is to balance. In skating, balance is hard because skaters must balance over a blade. These exercises can help skaters improve their balance.

Lifting a ball over your head during a double-leg squat will also strengthen your arms.

1. DOUBLE-LEG SQUAT: Squat back and down as if you are sitting on a chair. Lean your chest forward. Balance your weight between the heels and the balls of your feet, not on your toes.

2. SINGLE-LEG SQUAT: Stand with your arms extended out in front of you. Balance on one leg with the opposite leg extended straight forward. Squat down, keeping the opposite leg in the air. Rise to your original position. Repeat with the opposite leg.

3. SIDE SHUFFLES: Take a step sideways to the right with your right foot. Lift and place your left foot where right foot was. As your left foot comes down, take another step with your right foot. Now switch and go in the other direction.

core—muscles that control the lower back and tummy

flexibility—able to bend

endurance—the ability to keep doing an activity for long periods of time

center of gravity—the point at which a person's mass is evenly distributed in all directions

Chapter 4

Judging the Programs

A technical panel and a judging panel watch and score each team at competitions. A lead official, the referee, makes sure everyone follows the rules, including other officials.

The technical panel looks at the difficulty of the required elements and gives a point value for each element. The panel of judges looks at the quality of each required element and gives it a grade. The judges also give a mark for each of the five program components. The five components are skating skills, transitions, performance/execution, choreography, and interpretation of the music.

Judges have to pay close attention to performances.

Free Skate

Each team performs a free skate routine, also called a long program. Depending on the level of the team, the performance lasts up to 4 minutes 30 seconds. Beginning skaters have shorter routines, about 2 minutes long.

The number of elements varies from five to nine moves with transitions in between. During the long program, skaters must show expressions, emotion, and movement to the music. Synchronized skating is not only athletic, it is also artistic.

SHORT PROGRAM

Junior- and senior-level teams perform a second routine called the short program. It lasts 2 minutes 50 seconds and must contain five specific elements. The short program is all about performing difficult technical elements. The skaters are judged on their performance of those elements.

Before a competition, each routine is given a score based on how difficult it is. During the competition, the judges watch to see how well a team performs the planned routine. A more difficult routine can earn a higher score than an easier routine.

Team Hungary performs a junior-level short program.

Using Your Imagination

Skaters should listen to their music daily, says Coach Lynn Benson. She led one of the most famous synchronized skating teams, the Haydenettes, for 26 years. Benson tells skaters to go over the movements in their minds. She says to picture the performance in three ways — as a skater doing the routine, as a spectator watching, and as a judge.

Lynn Benson

Fast Fact

Russia's Team Paradise won back-to-back world titles at the World Synchronized Skating Championship in Colorado Springs, Colorado, in 2017.

Chapter 5

Competition Time

Synchronized skaters always match, from practice uniforms and competition outfits to the same hairstyles and makeup. What if a skater has bangs and the rest of the team does not? The bangs will be sewn into the skater's hair with a needle and thread. If the team members decide to have their hair pulled into buns, everyone has to have a bun. A fake bun will be added to any skater who does not have a real one, except the boys.

SMILE!

Another important part of presentation is expression. The skaters' smiles and body language need to match. Judges watch to make sure the expressions match the music. Smiles are important and should be on each skater's face.

Fast Fact

Don't step on the ice with a bobby pin in your hair or it could cause your team a **deduction**. Bobby pins and other hair holders that could fall onto the ice are not allowed.

deduction—points taken off a team's score

IN STEP

Synchronized skaters must have perfect footwork. One sloppy move could trip the other skaters and cause a chain reaction of falling. The skaters must move together. Dancers and pair skaters work to match one partner. Synchronized skaters must match up to 19 teammates. Teams are judged by how well they skate together and stay in formation.

WHEN TO LET GO

There are a couple of rules that synchronized skaters have to keep in mind during competition. Don't let go! That's why upper body strength is important, so the skaters can maintain their holds. A break in a line or a circle is disruptive. Skaters may not be able to get into position for the next move after a break.

But if a skater starts to fall, the rule changes to — let go! Dragging down your teammates because you are falling is not a good team effort.

Chapter 6

Notable Teams

Synchronized skating was called precision skating in 1956 when the first team was formed. Dr. Richard Porter, a professor at the University of Michigan in Ann Arbor, put together a team called the Hockettes. They entertained the crowd between periods during hockey games. The Hockettes still perform today.

GOING INTERNATIONAL

International competition for synchronized skating started in the late 1970s. The first official international contest was between Canadian and U.S. teams in Michigan in March 1976. Minneapolis, Minnesota, was the site of the first WSSC in 2000. Team Surprise from Sweden won the gold medal.

Finland and Sweden have dominated the top positions in synchronized skating. Finland has had three world champion teams that have won a total of 19 medals. Eight of their medals were gold. Sweden ranks second with 11 medals, six of them gold.

international—between or among the nations of the world

Fast Fact

In 2016, 26 teams competed at the WSSC held in Budapest, Hungary. It was the most teams to ever compete in the event.

Team Finland performs in 2016.

U.S. SUPERSTARS

Since synchronized skating is a team sport, there are no single superstars. But one U.S. team, the Haydenettes from Lexington, Massachusetts, has earned five WSSC bronze medals. The team has also won 24 U.S. National Championships. Every year for the last 16 years, the Haydenettes have represented the United States at the WSSC.

the Haydenettes

In 2007 the team from Miami University became the first from the United States to win a medal at the WSSC. The Miami University team brought home the silver medal. Three years later, the Haydenettes earned the second U.S. team medal at the WSSC when they won bronze.

THE OLYMPICS

Synchronized team skating is the only class of figure skating that is not an Olympic sport. As enthusiasm grows, synchronized skating could become an Olympic sport in the future. Support for the sport has spread on social media. Maybe by 2022, Olympic spectators in Beijing, China, will be watching a team of 20 U.S. skaters glide across the ice in perfect synchronization.

Fast Fact

In 2014 the International Olympic Committee added another way for skaters to earn gold medals with the Team Figure Skating event. Each team includes a woman, man, ice dancing team, and pairs team.

Glossary

agility (uh-GI-luh-tee)—the ability to move in a quick and easy way

center of gravity (SEN-tur OV GRAV-uh-tee)—the point at which a person's mass is evenly distributed in all directions

choreography (kor-ee-OG-ruh-fee)—the arrangement of steps, movements, and required elements that make up a singles skating routine

core (KOHR)—muscles that control the lower back and tummy

deduction (di-DUHK-shuhn)—points taken off a team's score

element (EL-uh-muhnt)—a required move in synchronized skating, including blocks, circles, wheels, lines, intersections, move elements, creative elements, no holds elements, spins, and pairs

endurance (en-DUR-uhnts)—the ability to keep doing an activity for long periods of time

flexibility (flek-suh-BIL-uh-tee)—the ability to bend

formation (for-MAY-shuhn)—the way in which members of a group are arranged

international (in-tur-NASH-uh-nuhl)—between or among the nations of the world

move in the field (MOOV IN THUH FEELD)—when the whole team performs a freestyle move, such as a spread eagle or spiral

parallel (PAH-ruh-lel)—an equal distance apart

precision skating (pri-SIZ-shuhn SKAY-ting)—the original name for synchronized skating

step sequence (STEP SEE-kwuhns)—a set of moves that follow one after the other

transitions (tran-ZI-shuhnz)—steps and movements that link the required elements in a routine

Read More

Barnas, Jo-Ann. *Great Moments in Olympic Skating.* Great Moments in Olympic Sports. Minneapolis: SportsZone, 2015.

Labrecque, Ellen. *The Science of a Triple Axel.* Full-Speed Sports. Ann Arbor, Mich.: Cherry Lake Publishing, 2016.

Throp, Claire. *Figure Skating.* Winter Sports. Chicago: Raintree, 2014.

Internet Sites

Use FactHound to find Internet sites related to this book.

Visit *www.facthound.com*

Just type in 9781515781868 and go.

Check out projects, games and lots more at
www.capstonekids.com

Index